KU-714-647

MARVEL

WHAT WOULD

HULK

DO?

A STUDIO PRESS BOOK

First published in the UK in 2021 by Studio Press,
an imprint of Bonnier Books UK Limited,
4th Floor, Victoria House, Bloomsbury Square, London, WC1B 4DA
Owned by Bonnier Books,
Sveavägen 56, Stockholm, Sweden

www.bonnierbooks.co.uk

© 2021 MARVEL

1 3 5 7 9 10 8 6 4 2

All rights reserved

ISBN 978-1-80078-030-9

Written by Susie Rae
Edited by Sophie Blackman and Saaleh Patel
Designed by Rob Ward
Production by Emma Kidd

The views in this book are the copyright holder's own and the copyright,
trademarks and names are that of their respective owners and are not intended
to suggest endorsement, agreement, affiliation or otherwise of any kind.

A CIP catalogue for this book is available from the British Library

Printed and bound in Italy

WORKING OUT...

HULK VERY GOOD AT WORKING OUT.
HERE IS HULK'S WORKOUT PLAN:

1. PICK UP TRUCK IN EACH HAND.
2. MAKE SURE TO BEND KNEES, LIFT TRUCK.
3. THROW IT AS HARD AS POSSIBLE.

HULK VERY STRONG, SO FOR PEOPLE
WHO ARE PUNY LIKE THOR, IT OKAY TO
START WITH SOMETHING LIGHTER,
LIKE CAR OR HELPFUL PASSER-BY.

MAKE SURE TO COOL
DOWN AFTERWARDS
BY UPROOTING SMALL TREE.

GETTING A HAIRCUT...

NO NEED TO PAY FOR FANCY
HAIRCUT — IT JUST GROW BACK.
HULK CUT OWN HAIR USING
UPSIDE-DOWN BOWL AND ENTHUSIASM.

IT LITTLE KNOWN FACT THAT
HULK IS EXCELLENT COOK.
EVERYBODY ALWAYS ASKING
FOR RECIPE FOR HULK'S MASH:

1. TAKE POTATO
2. HIT POTATO VERY HARD

A CLASSIC
DISH.

BUMPING INTO AN EX...

IT ALWAYS AWKWARD TO SEE
OLD FLAME WITH NEW PARTNER,
BUT HULK NEVER GREEN WITH ENVY.
IT IMPORTANT TO BE THE BIGGER MAN.

RECYCLING...

HULK IS EXPERT AT GOING GREEN. RECYCLING VERY GOOD FOR THE PLANET...

... SO HE USE OLD BITS OF FURNITURE OR EMPTY FOOD TINS TO THROW AT PEOPLE WHO USE TOO MUCH SINGLE-USE PLASTIC.

PEOPLE DON'T NEED TO TELL HULK — HULK ALREADY KNOW HE A VERY STYLISH PERSON. WHEN CHOOSING CLOTHES, IT BEST TO PICK A LOOK THAT SUIT YOU AND STICK TO IT.

HULK LIKE TO WEAR RIPPED PURPLE SHORTS BECAUSE THEY GO WITH EVERYTHING.

FACING YOUR FEARS...

HULK FIND IT BEST TO CONFRONT FEARS HEAD-ON. ALL HE NEED TO FACE FEARS IS BRAVERY, STRENGTH...

... AND ENOUGH GAMMA RADIATION IN BLOODSTREAM THAT HE MUCH SCARIER THAN EVERYTHING ELSE.

HOUSEWORK...

HULK OFTEN HAVE TO RENOVATE HIS HOUSE, AS IT GET SMASHED UP IN BATTLES WITH SUPER VILLAINS A LOT.

IF SOMETHING GET DIRTY, BEST SOLUTION IS TO BREAK IT AND WAIT FOR DR BANNER TO REPLACE IT WITH NEW ONE.

TEAMWORK...

WORKING TOGETHER AND ASKING
FOR HELP ARE IMPORTANT PART OF
ACHIEVING GOALS IN WORKPLACE.

HULK FIND THE OTHER AVENGERS VERY
USEFUL FOR TASKS LIKE PICKING UP THINGS
THAT HULK THROW, GIVING HULK NEW
THINGS TO THROW AND FETCHING SNACKS.

FINE DINING...

WHEN DINNER IS INTERRUPTED BY SUPER VILLAIN ATTACK, NICE RESTAURANTS USUALLY HAVE LOTS OF THINGS TO THROW.

CORRECT ETIQUETTE IS TO START BY THROWING CUTLERY ON OUTSIDE AND WORK IN — HULK WON'T EMBARRASS HIMSELF AND DO IN WRONG ORDER.

LIVING WITH ROOMMATES...

ONE OF MOST COMMON
ARGUMENTS WITH ROOMMATES
IS WHAT TEMPERATURE
TO KEEP HOUSE AT.

DR BANNER LIKE TEMPERATURE HOT.
HULK LIKE TEMPERATURE COLD.

COMPROMISE BY RIPPING THERMOSTAT
OUT OF WALL AND YELLING.

BUYING COFFEE...

COFFEE SHOP LIE, FLAT WHITE NOT EVEN FLAT, AND WHEN HULK SMASH CUP TO MAKE IT FLAT, THEY ASK HULK TO LEAVE AND NOT COME BACK.

DR BANNER NOT HAPPY ABOUT THIS, BECAUSE HE LIKE THAT COFFEE SHOP. HULK ADVISE HIM TO BE MORE SPECIFIC IN COFFEE ORDER.

FAMILY DISPUTES...

MOST FAMILY DISPUTES BEST RESOLVED BY HONESTLY EXPRESSING FEELINGS.

EVEN WHEN HULK ACCIDENTALLY TURNED COUSIN GREEN THROUGH BLOOD TRANSFUSION, FAMILY WERE MOSTLY VERY UNDERSTANDING.

BODY POSITIVITY...

HULK SORRY TO SAY, BUT OTHER PEOPLE WILL NEVER BE AS BIG AND STRONG AS HULK, WITH SUCH NICE GREEN COMPLEXION.

STILL, IT IMPORTANT TO RESPECT AND LOOK AFTER YOUR BODY...

... EVEN THOUGH IT NOT SIZE OF HULK.

DISAGREEMENTS WITH FRIENDS...

THOUGH IT COMMON TO FALL
OUT WITH FRIENDS SOMETIMES,
IT STILL VERY RUDE FOR IRON
MAN TO BUILD GIANT ARMOUR
JUST BECAUSE HE TOO PUNY
TO FIGHT ME WITHOUT IT.

OTHER MARVEL BOOKS...